J. TERRY JOHNSON

CRITICAL FACTORS IN

FUNDRAISING

*The Little Green Book
for Chief Executive Officers*

Foreword by
ANDREW K. BENTON

10

CRITICAL FACTORS IN

FUNDRAISING

10 Critical Factors In Fundraising
Copyright © 2011 by J. Terry Johnson. All rights reserved.

Editing by Kylie Lyons
Cover and Interior design by Kandi Evans

Published in the United States of America

ISBN:978-0-615-50794-1

1. Business
2. Fundraising
09.08.11

DEDICATION

This book is dedicated to the memories of James O. Baird and George S. Benson, two masterful leaders in Christian higher education, both exceptionally gifted fundraisers who mentored me in my early years of college administration.

ACKNOWLEDGMENTS

Although the skeletal outline of this book is my own creative work, many of the anecdotes that illustrate the principles were contributed by some of the best fundraising professionals I have ever known. I am grateful for their willingness to share their stories, allowing all of us the opportunity to learn from their extraordinary experiences and successful careers. Among those who offered illustrations were: Bob Walker, Texas A & M; Charles Runnels, Pepperdine University; Marty Willadsen, Missouri Sports Hall of Fame; and John deSteiguer, Oklahoma Christian University.

I also extend my thanks to two former colleagues at Oklahoma Christian University. Andrew

K. Benton, the current president and chief executive officer at Pepperdine University, was my assistant at Oklahoma Christian for ten years. He demonstrated signs of administrative brilliance from the first day he arrived on the job. His tenure at Pepperdine has been marked with major advancements for the University. I am especially grateful to him for writing the foreword to *10 Critical Factors in Fundraising*.

Guy J. Ross, Jr. is a friend who is "closer than a brother." He also enjoyed a thirty-plus-year career in Christian higher education, having led the development program at Oklahoma Christian for more than three decades. You will come to understand how valuable he was to me after reading the first chapter, entitled "Recruiting Your Partner." Guy has contributed anecdotes, critiqued drafts, and offered his best counsel as I have worked through the various stages of writing this book.

Finally, I wish to thank those gifted professionals who have supported me with their respective skills. A special tip of the hat is extended to Kylie Lyons, copy editor; Kandi Evans, layout and cover designer; and Shelley Sapyta and Holly Hughes, who handled the process of walking the manuscript through the various publishing stations at BookMasters.

CONTENTS

FOREWORD

The pages that follow are, in many respects, the story of my own introduction to the art of fundraising. For a portion of the story, I was there: serving at Oklahoma Christian University from 1974 until early in 1984. Even then I knew that Terry Johnson had the right instincts when it came to garnering support. Integrity, candor, friend-making, and stewardship are never out of season or favor.

I have often said that, "pound for pound," Oklahoma Christian had one of the finest, most productive fundraising teams I have ever seen. I stand by that boast, although I was merely a staff observer, but proudly so. Now, with a few years of experience (a total of thirty-five, as a matter of fact), I am often asked for advice in fashioning and leading a team of advancement professionals who can fund the dreams of a college or university. I can't do better than recommend my friend and mentor's book that you now hold in your hands.

I owe my career in higher education to the author. I owe many of my own "instincts" to what I saw as Terry Johnson inspired the confidence of truly remarkable men and women, otherwise far removed from a small, but deeply sincere college located in the Southwest. I marvel as I think about those he enticed to come alongside Oklahoma Christian and how they responded with heart and devotion.

For a new president or chief development officer, this is a story of what is, indeed, possible if you will devote yourself to hard work and authenticity in your relationship with those who can make your own leadership dreams come true.

Andrew K. Benton
President
Pepperdine University

INTRODUCTION

Nonprofit organizations are known for their insatiable appetites for gift dollars. The good they accomplish is sometimes overshadowed by endless appeals for more and more money. As soon as one funding campaign goal is met, the development staff is geared to launch another. The process mimics the proverbial dog that chases its own tail.

Although development work is often led by a professional staff and an army of volunteers, the ultimate responsibility for raising the dollars and balancing the budget falls squarely upon the organization's chief executive officer. This book has been written with that person squarely targeted within the crosshairs of each chapter. He or she may be known as the "president" or "executive director" or by some other title but, for simplification, I have chosen to identify the nonprofit's chief executive as its *president*.

Looking on philanthropy's brighter side, it appears that individuals, trusts, estates, foundations, and corporations are giving away more dollars year after year. Agencies that report charitable-giving statistics indicate that in recent years the annual sum given to charities and nonprofits in the United States exceeds $300 billion. As my grandchildren say, "That's a lot of *coin*." The upward trend speaks well of the virtues and the generosity of the American people.

A closer examination of these grants indicates that some are huge, each running into millions of dollars. Unfortunately, that doesn't make it any easier for most organizations to secure sufficient funds to operate their programs. As has always been the case, the better-known, well-established institutions get the lion's share of the philanthropic support, leaving the rest of us to scramble like a pack of hyenas, searching for the leftovers.

Having spent thirty-two years of my professional career pursuing the funds that were necessary to keep a small, church-related university afloat, I know something about development. For twenty-one of those years, I was president and chief executive officer of Oklahoma Christian University and served as its chancellor for another five years following the presidency. I can testify that competing for gifts to support operations, endowments, and capital improvements is perpetual warfare, utilizing a massive amount of shoe leather and the keenest of wits.

During my tenure at the university, we managed to survive the "oil bust" of the eighties, followed by the collapse of our local banking industry, resulting in massive layoffs and thousands of real estate foreclosures throughout the state. As if that were not enough misery, Timothy McVeigh and Terry Nichols drove a stake into the heart of our city on April 19, 1995, when their rented Ryder truck was used as an explosive device, reducing the Alfred P. Murrah Federal Building to rubble. For months after the tragic event, almost all available charitable gifts in our state were channeled to agencies designed to care for the surviving victims and families of those who perished in the explosion.

Those were not easy times for any of us in the Sooner State. Development staffs were forced to become more adroit in the art of fundraising, skillfully presenting appeals to an overtaxed pool of donors. Some charitable organizations had to close, while others had to scale back their operations. Had a few of their chief executives been able to master key elements found in this book, they may have been spared the embarrassment of losing their jobs.

Before plunging into the ten critical factors pertaining to fundraising, let me establish an essential premise upon which all development work is predicated. The success of any charitable organization is dependent upon two prerequisite elements being in place: *1) the organization must have a worthwhile mission,* and *2) it must employ a staff of competent people to advance its cause.* Your best efforts will eventually fail if these "givens" are not part of your equation for funding success.

I was privileged to lead a university that understood the niche role it served among institutions of higher learning and had outstanding personnel in the classrooms and on the management team to build the university's reputation. It would have been impossible to have achieved any measure of funding success if either of these elements had not been firmly in place. They are the starting blocks for any organization that seeks to have a great development program.

For those institutions that *do have an honorable mission* and *do employ talented people*, I am dismayed that so many are struggling to find the funds they need to operate. Presidents frequently appeal to their boards, *"I must have your support to hire a new development officer. We can't make it without an accomplished fundraiser."* Admittedly, there never appear to be enough talented development officers to staff the organizations that seek them, but I believe the issues preventing most institutions from reaching their monetary goals reside more often with their presidents than with their development staff.

Few people, outside of those who have served as chief executive officers, can fathom the stress that accompanies this position. The hours are long, the decisions are tough, and the responsibilities of the office fall heavily on a president's heart. Handling a regular diet of multitasking assignments produces a high "burnout" rate among presidents, often resulting in the board's search to hire a new top executive.

Each man or woman selected to serve an institution as its president brings unique talents and skill sets to the office. Having performed well in management or in an operational role, many are promoted from within their respective organizations. This being the case, it's easy for them to revert to tasks that are within their own comfort zones rather than learning correct fundraising principles and elevating development-related duties to a higher priority in their personal work schedules.

Presidents are busy people, constantly doing whatever they can to keep their enterprises moving forward. Novices in the office are tempted to delegate too many of the development tasks, learning too late that some of these fundraising assignments can only be handled by the chief executive officer. Eventually, a president who fails to perform productively in the development role will discover his board looking elsewhere for a new leader.

Someone else may wear the title, but every president is *de facto* the organization's "chief development officer." People who are capable of providing the most financial support for an organization usually want to spend time with its top leader. A president who hides behind others to get the fundraising job accomplished may be beloved by the students and held in high esteem by co-workers, but he or she is neglecting a vital function within the chief executive officer's job description. Other functions can be reassigned more easily than the job of presidential fundraising.

10 Critical Factors in Fundraising is a handbook designed to fortify a president in his challenge to set the institution's development agenda, encourage him to play a more active role in the advancement program, and give him reason to believe that he will be successful in reaping the harvest. Reading the book is nothing more than preparation. Only those who look thoughtfully into the ten chapters and make the necessary adjustments will enhance their chances of becoming successful presidents.

Read this book with an open mind and an open notebook. Jot down the ideas that resonate and teach your development team what you have learned and how you propose to become an effective player in the development process. Your leadership will make a difference.

J. Terry Johnson

1

RECRUITING YOUR PARTNER

I'm a big fan of Jim Collins and his blockbuster book "Good to Great." It is an excellent blueprint for taking a company, or any organization that employs people and manages an operation, from being good at what it does to becoming exceptional in its field. A key premise in the book is the concept: "You must get the right people on the bus." When it comes to running a development office, Collins's advice is pure gold.

And, by the way, "Congratulations!" You're the "search engine" to find your top development officer. This is not an assignment to be delegated. You don't need to form a committee that will only compromise your best intuitive judgment. You must riffle through lists of acquaintances, network with your peers, place a few calls, and be prepared to ask the tough questions. At most, you may have an assistant gather the résumés and keep the process orderly, but the task of choosing your partner in fundraising is totally your call. You must be comfortable with the process and willing to be held accountable for the outcome.

So, what qualifications are required to be a respectable fundraiser? Sam Walton, the legendary founder of Wal-Mart, would have made an exceptional chief development officer. He was visionary, able to see beyond the moment, dreaming of *what could be* with just a little hard work and a lot of heart. Mr. Sam met people well, using a smile to disarm the wary, and he mastered the gift of calling people by name.

One day, Sam and Helen Walton came to our home in Oklahoma City for a small luncheon party that my wife and I hosted in their honor. Having invited a few of the Waltons's friends to be our guests, we set the dining room table for ten. Using fresh vegetables harvested from her mother's garden and pan-frying chicken breasts to perfection, Marty, my wife, served a wonderful meal. It was down-home cookin' for a down-home kind of guy.

I had never met the Waltons until that day, but when Mr. Sam strolled up our sidewalk, I greeted him at the front door. "Why, Terry," he said with a broad smile on his face, "I've been looking forward to meeting you for such a long time." All of my pent-up anxiety disappeared. I immediately relaxed and, for the next hour and a half, thoroughly enjoyed the table discussion about the most common subjects—family, flying, and the good old days in Oklahoma. Sam Walton was a man "at ease" with himself, and that put others at ease as well.

That's where I would start in my search for a development leader. In sizing up a prospect, I would ask myself these questions:

- Who is this person without his or her mask?

- Is he uptight or open and relaxed?

- Is she comfortable making new acquaintances?

Some of the skill sets for a development officer can be taught, but there are a few qualities that need to be part of the DNA. Ask yourself some additional questions:

- Is this candidate a people-person?

- Can she make small talk? Is she a good conversationalist?

- Does he make a good first impression?

- Would I be comfortable working side-by-side with this person on a daily basis? Would we be a good team when making calls?

The job description is not for an office clerk with managerial skills; those you can find anywhere. What you're looking for is a person who can charm a crowd as effectively as former presidents Ronald Reagan and Bill Clinton did on their very best days.

There are a few critical questions you need to ask when checking with others about your candidate for the development position. These questions pertain to qualities that cannot be discerned easily in an interview. Dig below the predictable references in the résumé to find others who might provide a more objective assessment of the prospect's true qualifications. Then, ask:

- Is this person a self-starter, or will it be necessary for me to wind him up every day to get him out of the office?

- Does this person have sound judgment, and does she get along well with colleagues and the general public?

- Is this person willing to travel, enduring sixty-hour workweeks, or longer?

- Can I trust this person to be candid with me, yet remain loyal in his discretionary conversations with others?

A common trap when hiring development staff is to rely too heavily upon the candidate's self-proclaimed "experience" in fundraising. For someone to make a big deal about his or her "five years in the development office at Ajax University" may be code and correctly deciphered as: "I tried development for five years at Ajax. It didn't work out too well there; but hey, I'm willing to give it a go at your place." I would rather hire someone with no experience in fundraising if he or she has the right personality and temperament than to become "strike two" or "strike three" in some misfit's non-illustrious development career.

Most importantly, hire your top development officer from among those prospects with whom you can build a solid, professional friendship. This needs to be someone with whom you can spend many hours, working together and traveling days at a time without getting on each other's nerves. Your job is difficult enough as it is. It becomes impossible if you must "endure" the company of an incompatible bozo who is charged with making the dollars appear for your organization.

For virtually the entire twenty-one-year tenure of

my presidency, a college classmate, Guy J. Ross, Jr., was vice-president, and later senior vice-president, leading the development functions at Oklahoma Christian. My predecessor had hired Guy before I began my career at the university, so I make no claim about having discovered him. But when offered the presidency, I immediately conferred with Guy, asking him to work with me as the leader of our development office. Both in our early thirties, we grew up together on the job.

Here is what Guy did for me in his role as the chief development officer. First, *he made me laugh*. In a job that gets heavy at times, it's important to have a close associate who can bring a smile to the boss's face. Guy's humor came from his being an exceptional storyteller—an accomplished raconteur. That talent, by the way, makes for great table conversation when trying to warm up a standoffish donor prospect.

Second, Guy was exceptionally talented in *the art of soliciting gifts*. You would be surprised how many pseudo-development officers are great with the office management side of their position but completely inept at asking for the gift. They stir up the dust to hide their deficiencies but must eventually face their shortcomings in this competitive business of raising gift dollars.

Third, Guy was *a brilliant strategist*. He could read the subtleties of relationships we were developing with our donors and make the right calls when "moves" needed to be made. Many of the faculty and staff were rarely in a position to see him operate in this fashion, but I benefited daily from his wise counsel. The waters in development can become choppy at times, and the president needs a close ally to help steer the ship through narrow straits. It helps considerably if the chief development officer has some ability to read people, understanding what they feel about the appeal that is on the table, and knowing what corrections need to be made in order to secure the gift.

Many publications that address the leadership role of the president comment on the loneliness that accompanies the office. It's difficult for it to be otherwise. If the organization's top leader becomes too close to any member of the staff, he is open to the criticism of engaging in favoritism or cronyism, diminishing his effectiveness of being a leader that operates with fairness and equanimity toward all employees.

Although recognizing the principle of impartiality, I found that having *a close confidant* with whom I could share virtually any secret on the planet outweighed the critical voices of those who thought otherwise. Of course, this sounding board does not have to be the chief development officer, but a president needs someone within the organization to play that role. Confidants outside the immediate community rarely understand the subtle nuances that influence the political realities inside the organization.

Most importantly, Guy was the *consummate team-player*. We drew energy from each other, complementing each other's strengths and weaknesses. We worked together like the principal characters in Neil Simon's *The Sunshine Boys*. We were Brooks and Dunn, Martin and Lewis, Huntley and Brinkley, and yes, at times, Laurel and Hardy.

One afternoon in Manhattan, Guy and I were making a development call at the corporate offices of Metropolitan Life Insurance Company. We had been beating the New York City sidewalks for four days, with little to show for our efforts, and had just finished lunch before making our 2:00 p.m. appointment.

As was our normal pattern, I led the opening warm-up conversation. It was my responsibility to make the introductions and provide our host with appropriate background information about the university. When I completed the highlights of the current year, Guy was on cue to move into our appeal and then I would make the "ask" and close the visit. Only this time, as I concluded my opening remarks, there was silence from Guy. I quickly looked in his direction to discover that he was almost asleep, barely tracking what I had been saying for the past five minutes.

No problem, I thought to myself. *I know Guy's part as well as my own.*

So I turned to our corporate friend and promptly ran through the points Guy would normally have made. Somewhere toward the end of my spiel, Guy pulled himself together and began to make his best case for why Met Life should fund our proposal. It was virtually word-for-word what I had just told the man who was seated across the enormous desk. Our host was cordial, but we never got a dollar for our efforts.

I would not take a million dollars from Met Life for that moment we shared in their offices on that summer's afternoon. To me, it symbolizes the union that must exist between a president and his chief development officer. They must be a team. They must work as one. They must be on the same wavelength when it comes to raising the vital funds for their institution. Of course, it's best if they don't take naps during their solicitation visits.

So, as Jim Collins says, "Go out and get the right people on the bus." You must lead the effort to find that kindred spirit with whom you can work to shape the development program at your institution. Then, work in tandem with that person to see that the plan is well executed. It likely will be the most important appointment you make to your senior management team.

2

WIN WITH CONSULTANTS

In the summer of 1974, just a month or two before stepping into the ring of fire, I attended a conference in St. Louis for "new college presidents." The Council for the Advancement of Small Colleges, which later became known as the Council of Independent Colleges, hosted the workshop. Most of the men and women who attended had been serving as presidents of their respective institutions for one or two years. I had not yet found time to order new letterhead or business cards.

During one session of the workshop, the conferees took a personality profile assessment to determine their strengths and weaknesses as related to the responsibilities typically handled by chief executive officers. The assessment outcomes were displayed in circular graphs that were taped to a blackboard for all in the room to see. One by one, the facilitator began to examine the graphs, making observations about each of the respondents as he came to their respective graphs. We all knew when he was talking about our own results, but the graphs were not identified and names were never mentioned.

There was an awkward pause when the instructor began to interpret my graph. "My, my," he said as he studied the findings. "This person is somewhat of a social recluse. I'm afraid this person will find the presidency rather difficult unless he has an outgoing spouse who can carry part of the social load." *Whew!* Having a wife who excelled in social graces, I began to breathe once again. There was hope for me after all.

I share that story to make this point: None of us has all the tools we would like to have to succeed in the presidency. The role is far too demanding for anyone to master the skill sets and dispositional grace required to fulfill the complete spectrum of leadership responsibilities. Each of us brings strengths and weaknesses to the office. The key to our success is in knowing where we excel and where we have limitations. Then, we must compensate for our deficiencies.

The same assessment process is advisable as you examine your development team. You and your new chief development officer have collective strengths, each complementing the other, and the sum should be greater than the parts. But it is unlikely that your team can achieve the results you would like to have without some assistance from people who have special insights into key parts of your development program. Only the largest of organizations may be in a position to provide this expertise with permanent staff appointments. The rest of us, smaller and less experienced, must rely upon "consultants."

I confess to having had a jaundiced view of consultants in my early years. To me, they appeared to be expensive "know-it-alls" who spent too much time trying to impress the boss in order to justify their sizeable fees. My predecessor had used three different development advisers, each bringing his own special expertise to our advancement program. Throughout my tenure in office, I ended up using all three of these consultants and even added a fourth specialist for a major funding project. All of these, bear in mind, were used to help us raise more money for the university. I would have to say, each paid for himself many times over.

The Regionalist

Even institutions that are nationally acclaimed cannot know everything there is to know about all regions of the country. It is difficult enough to stay current with the donor base within our own local community, so why should any of us think we have the inside scoop on what is happening a thousand miles away where we have limited contacts and exposure? When it becomes important to raise more money from new neighborhoods, you would be well advised to retain a *regional consultant* who can establish a bridge between your institution and the targeted community.

One of the most memorable human beings I ever encountered was DeWitt Wallace, cofounder of *The Reader's Digest*. We met for lunch twice at the top of the Pan-Am building in Manhattan and on one other occasion at his offices in Pleasantville, New York. Well into his eighties, Mr. Wallace allowed me, a young, inexperienced, college president from Oklahoma and fifty years his junior, to capture his valuable time and tell him about the work we were doing with bright liberal arts students. For me to converse with Mr. Wallace was a mismatch of intellects, but he never gave me reason to feel my inferiority. He stands out in my mind as the epitome of "cream rising to the top." Prior to his death, he graciously funded endowed scholarships for some of our top-echelon students.

The initial contact with Mr. Wallace, and my first appointment with him in New York City, came through a *regional consultant*. He happened to have contacts that were able to secure an appointment for me with the legendary publisher. I could have written dozens of letters without ever getting an appointment with such an influential business leader. What I needed was a broker to make the arrangements and lend his influence on my behalf. This consultant did the same for me with other prominent executives and corporate foundations on the East Coast. Some of those contacts became long-term friends of the university.

The Capital Campaign Coordinator

From 1960 until 2000, Oklahoma Christian University conducted capital campaigns among the Oklahoma City corporate community on a once-every-five-year cycle. Most of the campaigns were to raise brick-and-mortar dollars that enhanced the university's presence within the local community. The public side of the campaign had a small window of time for solicitations—usually no more than three months. The behind-the-scenes work to get us ready for those campaigns was immense and required unique strategies and new office procedures that our full-time development personnel were not experienced at handling.

To address this challenge, the university contracted for the services of a capital campaign-consulting firm. They, in turn, assigned to us the specific person we had requested to manage these special campaign efforts. Although this gentleman changed consulting firms a time or two during that forty-year span, we always sought his whereabouts and asked that his current employer send him to Oklahoma City for our project. In my judgment, having the best possible person assigned to work with the capital campaign is far more important than the credentials of the consulting firm itself.

Using the campaign consultant also allowed us to keep our own development staff working in the areas where they were most effective. The consultant would help us enlist the local endorsement committee and volunteer leadership, arrange for meetings and public events, send out press releases to the media, design and produce printed materials, account for pledges and deposits, and manage the downtown office during the time the campaign was underway. This person accepted responsibility for about every role in conducting the campaign except soliciting donors for pledges—that part was left to the staff and volunteers. The contract term was usually for eight to twelve months, and then the consultant was off to another assignment.

Many firms are in business to operate capital funding campaigns. Do your due diligence. Ask for references and call the presidents of those organizations that have been serviced by the consulting company under consideration. Ask the references for specific names of consultants employed by that firm and then ask to interview two or three of those recommended before signing the consulting contract. The value is in securing the best possible person for your institution and the campaign you have prepared to launch. This working relationship requires a "good fit."

The Public Relations Consultant

From 1978 until 1982, Guy Ross and I crisscrossed the nation in an attempt to raise $15 million to construct and endow a hands-on, sixty thousand-square-foot economic education museum known as Enterprise Square, USA. When the smoke cleared, we had secured seven gifts of $1 million or more, and thirty-one additional gifts of $100,000 and up. Donors hailed from seventeen states and included individuals, foundations, and a significant number of corporations.

The project had its own intrinsic worth, but it also represented a breakthrough opportunity for the university to have its "fifteen minutes of fame" on the national stage. In order for this objective to be achieved, the project needed exposure in major journals and other national media outlets. I hardly knew where to begin, but I was pretty sure it would require an agency larger than the ones we used to generate publicity in Oklahoma.

After a few visits with major firms headquartered in New York City, Guy and I met a gentleman who was executive vice president for the Public Relations Department at Pepsi Cola's corporate offices in nearby Connecticut. To my surprise, this experienced executive was considering an early retirement, returning to his former home near Ada, Oklahoma. We struck a deal, calling on this seasoned publicist to conceive of and execute a plan, promoting the innovative new center from coast to coast. Being able to establish that relationship resulted in more doors being opened than I could possibly have imagined.

Through the efforts of this consultant, Enterprise Square, USA was featured on *The Today Show* and *CBS Evening News*. Feature articles appeared in *The Wall Street Journal*, *Southern Living*, and a host of other nationwide periodicals. The Disney Channel ran a segment, highlighting the cleverly designed economic education exhibits.

The consultant also fed the Associated Press and other wire services with articles and background material that appeared in newspapers in virtually every state of the Union. Radio hosts from major metropolitan cities interviewed our administrative staff and design team members, always mentioning the university in their broadcasts. We had a fine publications staff, but there was no way they could have tackled such a project with similar results. We needed expertise in these matters that was well beyond our own capability.

The Generalist

Without question, the most valuable consultant we ever retained at Oklahoma Christian was W. R. Brossman, a talented fundraiser in his own right, having served for many years as vice president of Colorado College in Colorado Springs. Once a month, for more than twenty-five years, this well-informed veteran flew to Oklahoma City where he spent one to three days in meetings with the Oklahoma Christian president and his key development staff, offering counsel regarding the funding and public relations priorities at the university. These were grueling "white board" sessions that made a huge difference in what our development team was able to accomplish.

The *consulting generalist*, coming from a different region of the country (and not from our own religious fellowship), could help us see the university as others saw us. That perspective is so valuable when making appeals to dispassionate foundation executives and corporate leaders. There were times when the truth was painful to hear, but it kept the university from making major gaffes with our more sophisticated donors.

The monthly visits also helped to set the president's personal development agenda for the next thirty days. Knowing that the consultant would be back a month later, and that I would be held accountable for what we had or had not accomplished, I was much more energized to perform my development tasks in a timely manner. The regular meetings kept me engaged.

The agenda for each month's meeting, usually prepared jointly by the president and the chief development officer, was all over the map. It could include current operational funding efforts, capital campaigns, strategies for specific cultivation or solicitation calls, and planning for special events or selecting donor recognition gifts. Sometimes we worked on press releases, publications, or just about anything remotely associated with development.

Although I did not always heed our consultant's advice, I benefitted greatly from what he had to say. He was a fountain of fresh ideas. Consultants must be allowed room to offer suggestions without feeling stifled by their clients. Listen to what they offer as you would look at the food being presented on a cafeteria line. You take what appeals to you and leave the rest.

Occasionally, a consultant will step outside his own area of expertise. Even the best professional may offer advice on a subject or regarding a constituency where his knowledge is limited. Recognize this for what it is and move on.

Let me offer this one point of caution as it pertains to consultants. Keep them out of sight from people who are unable to appreciate what they bring to the organization. This may include trustees who want to chop all operation expenses to the bone, failing to see the greater good that "fresh eyes" can provide. The list may also include "bean counters" in the business office that seek an unreasonable standard of justification for all new expenditures in the development office's operating budget.

You may want to pay for your consultants out of

capital fund budgets, which usually allow for some advance development costs to be repaid when the capital campaign revenues begin to be received. What is important is that your consultants be able to perform their work without local politics hampering their operations. The best way to do that is for you to help them maintain a low profile.

3

GENERATE MORE
OPERATING REVENUE

Once the development team has been recruited and a general consultant is under contract, it is critical that the key personnel participate in a thorough assessment to determine the best way to raise the most important money on the table—operating funds. No president has any greater pressure on him or her than to balance the annual budget and meet all payroll obligations. Fail in these areas and the "Exit" sign over your office door will begin flashing.

In most instances, you will find there is little glamour in attracting the day-to-day gifts that are required to keep your organization afloat. The work is often mundane, unappreciated, and offers little opportunity to make a fuss over anything except that, once again, the faithful benefactors contributed enough small gifts to make the year successful. With hardly enough time to catch your breath, the process begins anew.

There is no higher priority in your development program, however, than raising sufficient operating revenue to fund your core mission. Brick-and-mortar dollars are exciting because they lead to new construction, and endowments are always impressive additions to our financial reports; but, if all of our efforts are centered on capital gifts, it is, as someone once suggested, akin to "going to our graves in a Rolls-Royce." It all looks good on the surface, but we cannot survive without more operating income. Actually, many of the items we acquire with our capital campaigns end up adding an even greater burden to the operating budget.

Wise executives in the corporate community have learned the secret of generating "multiple streams of income" to beef up their company's annual revenues. Their primary product or service may produce a major portion of the company's annual income, but ancillary services can make the difference in whether the year has been profitable or not. General Electric is the classic case used in schools of business to make this point.

Fifty years ago, the brand name General Electric was automatically associated with small appliances, especially those found in the kitchen. They manufactured toasters and blenders and television sets. We all had at least one GE product somewhere in the house. The Fortune 500 Company still licenses the manufacturing of these popular lines, but consider, for a moment, the diverse ways in which General Electric produces income to feed its healthy "bottom line."

For starters, we all purchase GE light bulbs. That's a stream of income; but are you aware that General Electric is one of the largest manufacturers of jet engines? These are "big ticket" items that take GE far from the home-consumer market—into another revenue source. Have you ever been to Rockefeller Center in New York City, the home of NBC Universal, a subsidiary of General Electric? That's a totally different stream of income, generated by sales within the entertainment industry.

Add to these GE Money that finances consumer purchases and provides families with interest-bearing credit cards; GE Health Care, designed to offer the public a special form of health insurance; and GE Infrastructure, providing basic technologies for developing third-world countries, and you begin to grasp what it means to have *multiple streams of income*. The principle is simple enough. Now, if we can transfer the concept to our nonprofit organizations and make it part of our strategy for balancing the annual budget, our fundraising load might become more manageable.

Since retiring from the university, I have enjoyed consulting with a few clients, helping them conceive of fundraising strategies for their respective institutions. One such organization happens to be a church-related ministry that places missionaries in countries throughout South America. This team of dedicated workers has been operational for more than thirty years and has been highly successful in its primary program. As with many organizations, however, its programming is limited by its ability to raise sufficient sustentation income.

When this ministry first began, it was funded entirely from the mission budgets of two West Texas churches. After a few years, only one of the churches remained as the organization's annual benefactor. For all practical purposes, there was only one stream of income to support the work of recruiting, training, and placing these missionaries in the field. The ministry soon outgrew the resources available from the one congregation, and launching a new development program became essential to its survival.

Over the past seven years, Continent of Great Cities has implemented the "streams of income" concept to generate more annual operating cash, enabling the ministry to quicken its pace of operations. Having increased its operating income from $750,000 per annum eight years ago to more than $1.6 million today, the ministry has sent many more teams of missionaries into the major cities of South America to establish "lighthouse churches."

Specifically, the ministry now looks to more than *(a) four hundred individuals* to support the program annually. It also has *(b)* a *board of directors* whose members generously support the cause with their personal contributions. More than *(c) thirty-five churches* now include the ministry in their annual mission budgets. A few *(d) foundations* provide the ministry with operating support. And, recently, *(e) special fundraising dinners* in Abilene and Ft. Worth, Texas; Oklahoma City, Oklahoma and Nashville, Tennessee, have garnered new support for an emerging organization that is enlarging its circle of friends. The ministry has a small *(f) endowment*, but plans are underway to increase those capital assets in order to generate an additional stream of operating income.

Because operating funds represent "life blood" for the institution, it is in your best interest to have these dollars come from as large a pool of donors as possible. A temptation for fundraisers is to dig deeper and deeper into the same wells. There is nothing wrong with asking constituents to give annually, nor to ask that they consider raising their annual gift amount; but when we rely on just a few donors to provide exceptionally large gifts in order for the operating budget to balance, we skate on thin ice. Eventually, we will lose one or more of those donors, either by death or from a decline in his or her interest in our program. When that occurs, our balanced budget and our ability to meet the payroll are both in jeopardy.

One possible way of enlarging the donor base is through "direct mail." I know what many of you are thinking; I disdained the idea of outlandish appeals though direct mail as well, and for most of my years in the presidency, I refused to consider it as an option. One highly successful experiment has taught me, however, that I may have been wrong in my earlier assessment.

The effectiveness of using direct mail as a source of increasing operating funds is unmistakably related to the sophistication with which we approach the exercise. Most home-styled efforts are doomed to failure because they do not take into account many subtleties of this niche marketing appeal. The process is slow, even in the best of programs, and it can be expensive in its early stages. Impatience kills many efforts before they have a chance to prove their mettle.

Over time, however, it is possible to build a pool of "proven donors," previously "non-donors" who have chosen to make a contribution to at least one of our appeals for support. The percentage of "non-donors" who become "first-time donors" is always small, often not paying for the fishing expedition. But once a person has made one gift and has become part of the "proven donor" pool, the percentage of these friends that will give a second, third, or multiple times is much greater. Furthermore, because that pool of "proven donors" is small compared to the much larger pool of "non-donors," the cost of mailing to that group is materially less, enabling the net income to be considerably greater.

If you are interested in pursuing this method of fundraising, I offer these points of caution:

- *Outsource this service.* However tempting it may be, do not try to handle this operation by yourself. Consider several firms that specialize in direct-mail operations and contract with one of them for its professional services.

- *Be patient with the process.* You may need to feed the program for a year or two as you continue to build your "proven donor" base.

- *Maintain editorial control* over the content of the letters and the frequency of appeals to the same pool, but allow the professionals enough latitude to do their job. They know how to reap the intended results.

- *Look to this program only for the icing.* You will still need to bake the cake in the field, working hard with your best belly-to-belly development programs.

You likely will have development personnel and volunteers to help you raise the annual operating funds. The president might be asked to play a strategic role with the cultivation of some key donors and attend many of the special events, but you are burdened daily by other responsibilities of your office. More of your personal time will be required for the larger capital gift campaigns.

It is critical, however, that the development team senses your commitment to having a successful operational gift program, meeting its quotas and playing a vital part in balancing the budget. That may call for your being present at a weekly staff meeting to see where you can be of the greatest assistance to the team's ongoing efforts or participating with staff and volunteers in an occasional phone bank callout to solicit operating gifts and pledges.

The organizations that are most successful in raising operating funds are usually well staffed with volunteers. Think of the effort put forth each year to make the United Way appeal a winner in your own community. The leadership for that group specializes in having volunteers put peer pressure on one another to reach the annual funding goal. Capturing the attention of the right group of volunteers (especially those who also qualify as donor prospects) will pay huge dividends.

Successful operational funding groups also emphasize the "good that can be accomplished" by donor participation. They almost always sell the *opportunity* rather than the *need*. Focus on the Family comes to mind. Rarely do you hear Dr. James Dobson laying a burden on his audience because his ministry's funding is low. To the contrary, he touts the good being accomplished by the gifts that pour into his mailboxes in Colorado Springs.

Whenever possible, secure multiple-year pledges from your general donor base. It keeps you from wearing out your welcome with annual solicitation calls. My best counsel is to use three-year pledges for operating gift campaigns and five-year pledges on major capital programs.

Finally, be cautious about launching a capital campaign prematurely. On the one hand, you cannot afford to wait until the operational budget is on "Easy Street," because you will never feel that you have enough operating gifts. But to initiate a capital campaign with little regard for how it might damage the operational support is shortsighted. At the very least, build into your capital campaign a generous amount of operational expenses so that the first dollars received on the capital campaign go to relieve the operating budget. If this is not done, you may find the capital campaign taking gift dollars away from the annual fund.

4

THE ART OF MAKING FRIENDS

A key component in any successful development program is the *cultivation process* that encourages donors to see themselves as friends of the institution. Rarely do donors give to a charity without embracing its fundamental mission, but the tipping point that determines to whom and how much they give is often wrapped up in the axiom that "friends give to friends." The president plays a key role in creating the friendship factor between the organization and its major donor base.

One of the most remarkable educators of the Twentieth Century was George S. Benson. Although small in stature, he had the heart of a stallion. Born in Oklahoma, Benson spent ten of his early adult years as a missionary in China before devoting himself to a professional career in Christian higher education. An outspoken proponent for conservative causes, Benson served twenty-nine years as president of Harding College in Searcy, Arkansas, stepping aside in 1965 to become the college's chancellor.

What is not widely known about Dr. Benson is that he also served ten years as chancellor of Oklahoma Christian College, eight of those years running concurrently with his presidency at Harding. To this day, it is the greatest example of unselfish, professional courtesy I have ever witnessed. On Mondays, Dr. Benson would crawl into his small airplane, leaving his home in Searcy, for his weekly fundraising trip to Oklahoma.

Now, here is where the story becomes bizarre. When Oklahoma Christian decided to move its campus from Bartlesville to Oklahoma City, Dr. Benson enlisted the support of community leaders in the state's capital to fund the move. Many of these Oklahomans had been dear friends of Dr. Benson, and they had become annual contributors to Harding College. Fully aware of the consequences of his actions, Dr. Benson encouraged his friends to shift their loyalties to the new school that was opening its doors in Oklahoma City.

Among those civic supporters who counted Dr.

Benson as a close friend were E. K. Gaylord, owner and publisher of *The Daily Oklahoman* and *The Oklahoma City Times*, and his son, Edward L. Gaylord. Both men had made modest gifts to Harding College and its National Education Program. Over the next three decades, however, these two families gave millions of dollars to Oklahoma Christian University. E. K. Gaylord and Edward L. Gaylord, both now deceased, also left generous testamentary bequests to the university. In doing so, they honored the wishes of their good friend, George S. Benson.

I cannot begin to calculate the man-hours James O. Baird and I spent developing heartfelt friendships with members of the Oklahoma City business community. Three generations of the Gaylord family served with their peers on the Board of Governors, a group of business leaders who aided the university in its many advancement programs. Honorary degrees were bestowed upon the family members and buildings were named in their honor. These are typical gestures of a university expressing its appreciation for donor generosity. We call this type of activity *recognition*, which is part of any organization's *donor cultivation process.*

But to describe the interaction between the Gaylord family and the university's presidents in such clinical terms would be to miss what was happening in building the relationships. This was not just about business or soliciting another gift. These points of contact grew into solid friendships. When E. K. Gaylord died in the spring of 1974, James O. Baird was on a church-mission assignment in Vietnam. He caught the first flight home and was present to officiate at Mr. Gaylord's funeral.

Similarly, I worked resolutely to procure Edward L. Gaylord's support of our capital campaigns at the university. But our relationship grew beyond our business association—the two of us becoming genuine friends. We met frequently in the afternoons for coffee, spending the time talking about our children, politics, or athletics. Our wives made out-of-town trips together to shop at boutiques and to enjoy lunch with mutual friends. We called one another in the late afternoons just to see if we could meet for supper, and at Christmastime, we exchanged gifts. We regarded one another as friends.

A typical mistake many of us make in our development activities is to rush the cultivation process. We press the issue of getting our agenda on the table without ever allowing the donor to share what may be on his or her mind. Being a good listener is a valuable asset for anyone, but it is especially useful to those of us engaged in fundraising. We may pick up critical information that can help us as we move toward the inevitable "ask."

Early in my career, I was trying to talk Stanley S. Kresge into flying from his home near Detroit, Michigan, to Oklahoma City, where we planned to celebrate the seventy-fifth birthday of a mutual friend and former Minnesota Congressman, Dr. Walter H. Judd. Mr. Kresge wasn't sure his health would allow him to fly commercial airlines, so I offered to pick up the tab for a small chartered jet just to ferry him back and forth from Michigan. I justified the charter on the basis of the old adage, "You have to spend money to make money." But still, it was a big-ticket item for a small, church-related college to absorb in its annual budget.

To my delight, Mr. Kresge accepted the offer. Then, he threw me a curveball that was unexpected. He asked if the plane could return him to Michigan by way of North Carolina, where he needed to make a visit to his friend Dr. J. Terry Sanford, president of Duke University. What could I say? "No, you are on your own when it comes to North Carolina!" That big-ticket item just got a lot bigger, costing me much more than I had originally bargained.

Somehow these things have a way of working out. I made numerous trips over the years to see Mr. Kresge at his offices in Troy, Michigan. We attended

Rotary Club meetings together, listened to nationally renowned speakers at Detroit's Economic Club, and enjoyed participating in local prayer breakfasts with his friends. He even introduced me to ginger sundaes at his favorite ice cream parlor.

Stanley and Dorothy Kresge gave almost $2 million of their personal estate to the university and influenced additional grants from the prestigious Kresge Foundation. Was it textbook development work, or friendship? Sometimes the two are hard to separate. What I have found is that donors have a greater willingness to make gifts to institutions that are led by their friends, especially if that friendship is genuine.

One of the best "friend-builders" I have met in university circles is Bob Walker, the legendary development executive from Texas A&M University. During his illustrious career, spanning the tenures of several university presidents, Bob has raised hundreds of millions of dollars from alumni and other donors with whom he has built solid friendships.

Bob tells the story of having lunch with an Aggie alumnus in Ft. Worth one day when he learned of a bachelor who owned a beautiful ranch in the Texas Hill Country. The rancher lived far enough off the beaten track so that few people ever bothered him with solicitation appeals. Bob secured the gentleman's name and address and set up his first appointment for a visit.

Over the next three years, Bob made frequent calls on this new acquaintance, often bringing him homemade brownies and a generous supply of Texas barbeque. He took some of his office colleagues with him, always being sure they dressed appropriately in blue jeans and boots. The highlight of each trip was a tour of the 6,700-acre ranch.

After solidifying his friendship with the potential donor, Bob invited the university's president to accompany him on a visit. The three men, riding in the owner's pick-up, covered all sections of the ranch. The rancher asked the president to ride with him in the front seat so he could help open the many gates along the way. The president's humility deeply impressed the rancher. He said, "Bob, you know it isn't every day that the president of Texas A&M opens gates for me."

The ranch, valued at $20,500,000, has now been deeded to the university with a life-estate reserved for the donor. Bob and the rancher continue to be close friends, a blessing that both men treasure.

Much of your friend-building activities will come at mealtime. A good development officer and a development-minded president will fill their calendars with breakfast, lunch, coffee, and supper appointments with those people who share an interest in the organization's core mission. On many of these occasions, the priority is not to solicit a gift, but to deepen the friendship.

I must hasten to add, however, that a development officer who constantly avoids making an "ask" may need to look for a different line of work. Eventually, he must let his friends know what they can do to help. Or, as my colleague Guy Ross likes to say, "Sooner or later, you have to spend some of the equity you have built up with the donor prospect."

I have become a fan of Terry Axelrod's philosophy of fundraising, described in her book "Raising More Money." A key element in her development strategy is the "P.O.E."—a "point of entry" meeting with people who know little or nothing at all about the charitable organization. These nonthreatening sessions are designed to introduce new friends to the organization without any hint of soliciting a gift. Those who attend the P.O.E. meetings may be added to the mailing list, perhaps seen in other settings, and, in time, invited to an "ask event" where a formal solicitation is made on behalf of the charitable institution.

What impresses me is how easy it is to expand the potential donor base through these brief introductory meetings. People will bring their friends because they know that no one can get hurt. Your friends become my friends, and we all end up working to advance the cause that knits us together.

Cultivation of new and existing friends is demanding work, and not always the easiest part of our development assignment. It takes patience. It takes thoughtful, purposeful action. It often comes with a price to be paid from our private life. But donor cultivation is absolutely essential to a well-designed advancement department. Without cultivation, we may as well throw darts at our donor list to see who needs their pockets picked today.

Charles Runnels and his wife, Amy Jo, deserve highest honors in the Development Officer Hall of Fame. Years ago Pepperdine University President M. Norvel Young and Executive Vice President William Teague enticed Charlie to leave his position with Tenneco Oil Company and begin a new career with the Christian liberal arts university. Charlie became a formidable player on the team that moved Pepperdine from its Los Angeles campus near Watts to its current site, overlooking the Pacific Ocean and the beautiful Malibu beaches.

One of Charlie and Amy Jo's early assignments was to work closely with Mrs. Frank (Blanche) Seaver, a wealthy widow whose $100 million-plus estate has greatly blessed the university's efforts to build a first-class academic program. The Runnels, being sincere people, approached their work with pure motives and did their best to become a true friend to Mrs. Seaver. She loved them, as they did her. But the demands placed upon the Runnels's personal lives to squire Mrs. Seaver to this dinner party or that concert and see that all was done in a way that suited Mrs. Seaver was almost more than anyone could be expected to handle. For years the Runnels performed their task with grace and humility, and it all worked out well for Mrs. Seaver and the university. It is a classic case of what friends will do for friends.

5

WHY SPECIAL EVENTS
ARE SO SPECIAL

Almost everyone enjoys a good party. We relish the food, delight in the fun, and leave with good feelings toward our hosts. Since a major assignment of the chief executive officer is to generate goodwill for his or her organization, it only makes sense that we spend time and money hosting our friends at some memorable events.

Throwing a good party, however, is not nearly as easy to accomplish as one might imagine. It takes creative planning, attention to detail, and flawless execution in order to achieve the intended results. For every impressive special event I have attended, I have been to twenty that were anywhere from *so-so* to downright *lousy*.

Impressions, good and bad, are made on guests who attend our dinners, graduations, seminars, and other public events. The people with personal wealth are making subtle judgments about our institutions as they attend these functions. Most of them have seen it all when it comes to staged presentations. They cannot keep from making mental comparisons about various charitable organizations and the messages being conveyed at their public gatherings.

What passes as a special event is not necessarily determined by the number of guests attending. Small, private dinner parties can be as beneficial to an institution as a massive dinner gala at the city's convention hall. The key to having had a successful event, whether large or small, is whether the *right people* were in attendance, and did the organization make a favorable impression upon these guests at the event?

Nothing is more disappointing than to go to great lengths to plan a party and have only a few guests attend. We have wasted the opportunity, not to mention valuable time from our staff and volunteers. So, what can be done to *attract the right crowd*?

For starters, our respective institutions will need to build good databases of potential guests, categorized for easy screening when sending out invitations. Computers allow us to do so much more in this area than was once possible, but there is still the human element that must keep the lists current and under constant review. Donors do not respond well when their names are misspelled, their addresses are wrong, or we fail to address them by the name they prefer.

I have become a strong believer in using some form of the "table captain" invitation method to secure the maximum audience for a dinner event. A printed invitation in the mail can only achieve a limited draw at the box office. What really packs people in is "word of mouth." When someone I know invites me to come with them to a program, I am far more likely to attend.

Here is where alumni, boards and councils, and other groups of institutional friends can make a significant difference. Their personal invitation means more than our own. Empower your volunteer groups and watch the attendance at your events begin to grow.

Looking over years of attending special events hosted by my own institution as well as many others, I offer this list of questions that should be asked by the chief executive officer or his designee who chairs the planning committee.

- Does the type of event we are planning provide the institution with the best opportunity to achieve its development objectives with the target audience?

- Is the venue the best possible location for this event, and does the room itself allow us the opportunity to connect favorably with our guests?

- Are the "right people" being invited to this event, and what can we do to be sure they attend?

- Do we have the best mix of entertainment, information sharing, and emotional electricity to make the right impression upon the audience?

- Have we chosen the very best emcee for the occasion?

- Do we have the "right people" seated with our own best impression-makers?

- Can we keep this program within a reasonable time limit?

- Are the printed materials, room decorations, food, entertainment, and audio-visuals the best quality we can possibly offer?

- Is there an available speaker or entertainer who will help us draw an audience?

- Do we have a donor that would underwrite the cost of the event, ensuring that all gifts from our attendees will go directly to our core program?

This list could go on for pages. I suggest these questions as representative of the interest the chief executive should manifest in the planning of any public event. Taking a carefree attitude is to waste an opportunity to showcase the organization and to advance its mission.

You must exercise special care in selecting an appropriate speaker or entertainer. The Oklahoma City Chamber of Commerce is the "best in the West" when it comes to putting on public relations events. Their capable staff can orchestrate a luncheon or dinner down to the smallest detail. They know how to "wow" an audience with just the right combination of business, breaking-news announcements, and first-class entertainment, including the sizzle that leaves guests feeling good about their decision to attend the party.

Even the best, however, can blow an event by choosing the wrong speaker. One night, at an important dinner designed to salute all former presidents of the local Chamber, a nationally known comedian was selected to entertain the packed house. The evening was a disaster. The comedian was profane, crass, and insulting to the very people he was expected to entertain. Before he had finished his performance, almost a third of the audience had left the building. The Chamber president issued an apology in the local newspaper a day or two later. Choose well for these occasions, or be prepared to pay the consequences.

Institutional posturing is critical at special events. No one likes to hear us whining or complaining about hard times. Admittedly, there are a few donors who reward an organization's "save our ship" message, but far more will respond to its vision of hope and its illustrations of success. Tell your institution's story passionately, but with the least amount of self-adulation possible, and you will make many friends in the process. A few choice words from a young person or a beloved staff member may have greater impact on the audience than a canned speech from a noted celebrity.

When hosting a special event, the right venue adds significantly to the occasion. The National Cowboy and Western Heritage Museum in Oklahoma City operates one of the best galleries of western art to be found anywhere in the nation. With bronzes by Frederick Remington and Charles Russell, watercolors and oils from more recent artists James Boren and G. Harvey, the galleries celebrate the American cowboy and his unique role in settling the West. Each year the museum attracts thousands of visitors who tour the galleries and exhibits, always leaving a few coins at the museum and its attractively appointed gift shop.

Much like their "cousins" at the Chamber of Commerce, the National Cowboy and Western Heritage Museum staff knows how to throw a great party. They combine good food, talented musicians, stunning art, and noted celebrities to draw a five-star, elite guest list for their dinners and public forums. Presidents, Hollywood stars, rodeo cowboys, and nationally acclaimed artists have all made their way to the fabled museum on Persimmon Hill.

For years, however, the museum had everything going for it except a room large enough to seat a sizeable audience. That deficiency was eventually addressed with a capital campaign, enabling the museum to build a first-class banquet room. Now, not only does the exhibition hall host more spectacular public events of their own, but their galleries provide the backdrop for many other groups that choose to rent their Great Hall.

Continent of Great Cities, the mission ministry cited earlier, recently hosted two of the most memorable fundraising dinners I have ever attended. The first was a dinner cruise held on the General Jackson Showboat that floats the Cumberland River in Nashville, Tennessee. Pat Boone was the evening's celebrity entertainer. Four hundred guests enjoyed the novelty of using the riverboat for the "ask event." It was a welcomed change from the normal dinner at a hotel ballroom.

The second event, held a year later, was at Nashville's new Schermerhorn Symphony Center. Again, four hundred guests attended the dinner concert, in part to hear about the ministry's work in South America, but also to catch a glimpse of the new music hall, which had been the talk of the town for months leading up to its grand opening. Take some time to be creative in choosing a venue for your development events; it will pay dividends.

Lest you believe that all good development events must feature a banquet, let me share the story of an unusual nonprofit organization that garners a significant portion of its annual income from hosting golf tournaments. The Missouri Sports Hall of Fame in Springfield operates a hands-on museum honoring exceptional athletes, coaches, and teams that have achieved high honors in the Show-Me

State. Jerald Andrews, the Hall's president and chief executive officer, and Marty Willadsen, vice president, comprise one of those remarkable teams that make development work look fun.

In addition to hosting an annual enshrinement dinner with as many as 1,800 patrons in attendance, the Missouri Sports Hall of Fame schedules between fifteen and twenty charity golf tournaments in all parts of the state. Golf outings require considerable time spent by the staff to secure sponsors, arrange sites, enlist participants, and ensure appropriate publicity for the events. But the benefits are many-fold. In some instances, major donors to the Hall were introduced to the organization by playing in one of its tournaments.

Some of your best events will become annual traditions. If your donors were truly entertained at last year's function, they will anticipate the next dinner or public forum and may invite friends to join them. Build on the success of your traditions, but try not to allow them to become stale. Post-event assessment sessions will keep you on track.

Good planning and meticulous care to preparation will make special events the cultivation tool you want them to be. There is no magic formula—just hard work. When everything is running on all cylinders, you will get leveraged benefit from the dollars spent. Your prospective donors will have had a shared experience that will advance your cause just about as rapidly as any other use of your development department's limited operating budget.

6

CAPITAL IDEAS FOR A CAPITAL CAMPAIGN

Once the operational funding machine is running on all cylinders, it's time to consider a capital gifts campaign. If you allow too many years to pass without offering your donor base an opportunity to step up to a higher giving level, you're leaving dollars on the table. These same friends will choose to make their larger gifts to other organizations that appear to have a special need for capital funds.

Donors choose to make gifts to charitable organizations for many different reasons. With most, the motive is pure altruism; they give to a cause, expecting nothing in return except the satisfaction of knowing that their gift is helping to make a difference. May their numbers greatly increase!

However, for a capital campaign, those same donors will usually make much larger gifts than they have contributed to the annual fund. A couple that gave $5,000 for the operating budget may give $100,000 or more to a well-scripted capital fund appeal. They still believe in the organization's mission and will contribute annually to its support, but they have been challenged to think in bigger terms because of the special appeal that invites a larger, more sacrificial gift.

In structuring a capital campaign, the first requirement is to determine the case statement for making the funding request. What are the current capital improvement opportunities? Do they include new construction? The remodeling of existing facilities? Property acquisition? Endowments? Debt reduction? Major equipment? All of these represent big-ticket items that usually require a capital campaign.

Although it is appropriate to have a capital campaign for a single project (e.g., a new science building or endowed scholarships), I prefer the "omnibus campaign" that gives donors and development staff an opportunity to match mutual interests. Nothing is more frustrating than to be turned down by one or more of your very best prospects because the organization tried to force-feed its single most important project down the throat of the donor clientele. With the omnibus approach, there is usually something on the smorgasbord table that looks appealing to each donor's personal appetite.

The omnibus campaign also allows the organization to cast a broader vision for what it is doing and where it is going. Having multiple projects that need to be funded suggests, *We are moving forward on several different fronts*. As each piece of the campaign is completed, celebration occurs, and that fuels the staff and volunteers to get other elements fully funded.

To be sure, omnibus does not mean "everything we can think of, including the kitchen sink." That type of campaign has no sense of urgency and will be perceived by the public for what it is: a blue-sky wish list. Tuck that list under your pillow at night and see if the Tooth Fairy will take care of it.

What is meant by *omnibus* is a collection of three or four key undertakings, all deemed ready for implementation, and offering a solid rationale for each. Perhaps the case statement describes the urgency for constructing a new building, and funding some well-defined endowments, and even providing a modest amount of start-up funds for a new venture. These elements are packaged and sold as being the most crucial needs the institution has at this moment in time.

A good starting point for an omnibus campaign is to have the charitable organization conduct a self-study. This exercise may take months to complete, but it is time well spent. A proper self-study should involve staff members and friends working together to assess the institutional strengths and weaknesses. Once determined, it should become clear where capital funds are most needed. The study provides the president with a mandate from which he or she can mount the "bully pulpit."

A few months before assuming the president's post, I made a visit to Princeton, New Jersey, where I called upon Dr. George Gallup, the famous pollster and founder of the Gallup Organization. My mission was twofold: first, to engage Dr. Gallup's firm in conducting an attitudinal survey among a nationwide sampling of college students; and second, to ask that he personally deliver the survey's findings at our commencement exercises the following year. Dr. Gallup graciously accepted both assignments.

The student study was funded by a small grant from the Pew Charitable Trust in Philadelphia. Specifically, the survey was to determine collegiate student attitudes pertaining to social, economic, and political issues, covering topics that ranged from the Vietnam War to feelings about big business. Dr. Gallup broke his findings on our campus in the spring of 1975.

The message that reverberated from the Gallup Poll was that college students, at the close of the Vietnam War and in the aftermath of the Civil Rights movements, were in an anti-establishment mood. They held government officials suspect but viewed the barons of American business with even greater contempt. Although the students were moderately well versed in the workings of our nation's social institutions and government bodies, they had universal ignorance about the important role free enterprise played in their everyday lives.

Armed with this powerful information from Dr. Gallup's poll, I was aware that higher education was failing to teach the rudimentary principles of our economic heritage, but I felt as inconsequential as an ant dancing on a football field to find a solution. "What could one relatively small, church-related college in Oklahoma do about this overwhelming educational deficiency?" That question, begging for an answer, became the rallying cry (the "case," if you will) for the nationwide campaign that provided $15 million to build and endow Enterprise Square, USA.

Once the capital campaign's purpose has been established, the president and the development team must use that clearly articulated case statement to enlist the support of volunteer workers at the highest possible level. These leaders, if well chosen, will be helpful in enlarging your organization's sphere of influence. Some of the volunteers' friends will be attracted to your capital funding projects, and, of course, the workers themselves will be likely donors to the campaign. Gaining top-level volunteers will not, in itself, secure your success, but failing to get this job done in advance of the campaign will, most likely, ensure your failure.

William F. Martin, chairman and chief executive officer of Phillips Petroleum Company, accepted the chairman's role for the Enterprise Square, USA, funding campaign. Phillips Petroleum was the largest publicly held company headquartered in Oklahoma at that time. If the innovative educational museum had any chance of getting off the ground, it would require that Phillips Petroleum be fully engaged.

Mr. Martin was exemplary in his leadership role. He secured a $2 million pledge from Phillips Petroleum to help launch the campaign. Using the company's magnificent Gulfstream jet aircraft, Mr. Martin flew Guy Ross and me to business luncheons in Los Angeles and New York City, where we met with his friends and business associates and made our appeal. He enlisted some of those same friends to join him on a National Round Table for Enterprise Square, USA, and from that group, and a few key friends of the university, more than $15 million was pledged. He handled the role of campaign chairman in textbook fashion.

A new sophistication is required of the development team as it begins to solicit the larger gifts. Some donors will choose to use charitable trusts or other testamentary instruments to fund their pledges to the campaign. You and your staff will need to work with accountants and attorneys to guide the donors through the maze of options in order to find the appropriate vehicle for each situation. Your donors have some weighty questions on their minds:

- "What are the tax implications of my gift?"

- "Will I get the full charitable deduction this year?"

- "Are there ways to structure the gift to enhance my tax write-off?"

Moreover, there are non-tax issues that may come into play in the donor's decision to make a larger gift.

- "What opportunity do I have to 'leave some tracks in the sand' with my gift?"

- "What are my peers doing in response to this campaign?"

- "With this gift, will I be in a position to have greater voice in the direction of the organization?"

- "Will I be extended an invitation to serve on the board?"

- "Will I be invited to attend special functions normally reserved for a small number of influential donors?"

The list is practically endless. It does behoove the development team, however, to get inside the donors' heads in order to know what preparation needs to be made prior to making the appeal. When large gifts and estates are being solicited, more warm-up time is usually in order.

Frank Tolbert lived in a small cinderblock house in Muskogee, Oklahoma; drove a twenty-year-old Ford LTD; and wore old, tattered clothes practically every day. Although he lived just above the poverty line, Frank was an intelligent man who had an accounting background; but by all appearances, he had nothing to give to any charitable organization.

Over a period of several years, John deSteiguer, chief development officer for Northeastern State

University in Tahlequah, Oklahoma, spent many hours visiting with Frank Tolbert in his humble home. The two men found topics of common interest, exploring them conversationally, and they forged a friendship that was genuine and reciprocal.

Although John wondered on occasions whether he was spending his time wisely, he listened carefully to Frank's story and waited patiently for the right cue. One day Frank asked John to prepare some bequest language that could be submitted to Frank's attorney. Less than a year following Frank's death, Northeastern received a bequest that, combined with some matching funds from the State of Oklahoma, exceeded $850,000. Larger gifts take time and a higher degree of sophistication when estates are involved, but they can certainly be worth the effort.

Once the decision has been made to launch a capital campaign, the case has been articulated, and volunteer leadership enlisted, it is show time. You are ready for liftoff. The time has come to see if you can communicate your organization's dream to the public, winning their favor with checkbooks in hand. Read on!

7

SUCCESS IS IN THE APPROACH

There's a catchphrase going around today that says, "The success is in the follow-up." It's hard to argue with that axiom. Many opportunities have been missed because of the failure of a salesperson to follow up with a customer.

Taking nothing away from the necessity of good follow-up, I would propose that your success may just as well be determined by your *approach* to the donor. The follow-up will make little difference if the donor declines to set an appointment in the first place. Everything we have discussed up to this point may be categorized as "saddling up" activities. *Our real work begins with the approach.*

When calling upon corporate and foundation

donors we often encounter those troublesome gate-keepers. They have a difficult job. Their bosses have asked them to screen out certain callers and visitors, and that often includes people who are seeking donations and capital gifts. In some cases, it becomes necessary to court the executive's assistant before you can begin the cultivation process with the grant-maker himself.

One of those gatekeepers I remember fondly was Beverly Buben, the talented executive assistant for Sam Noble, chairman of Noble Affiliates, Inc., with offices in Ardmore, Oklahoma. While maintaining a cordial disposition on the telephone, she was one of the best I have seen at protecting her boss from nuisance calls. If I wanted to see Mr. Noble, I was at the mercy of Ms. Buben.

Over the years, I learned how to spend just a few minutes of each call visiting with Ms. Buben about those topics of special interest to her. We chatted about her daughter, Sherri, who eventually enrolled at Oklahoma Christian, played basketball there, and would become the women's basketball coach at the University of Oklahoma (Sherri Buben Coale). Only then would I ask to speak with Mr. Noble or see about setting up an appointment. Treating her with appropriate respect acknowledged that she was a person in her own right. That alone can make a big difference when it comes to getting an appointment with a gatekeeper's boss.

As a general rule, and whenever possible, I made the effort to go to the top of the command center when getting my appointments. Seeing the chief executive officer was much better than working through the lower ranks where each decision had to be reviewed by someone's superior officer. Occasionally, there were bruised feelings for having gone over the head of a junior officer, but I found that this risk was worth taking. Chief executive officers make decisions on the spot and are not constrained by the same ceilings that other staff members have to observe when making their grant decisions.

Donald Procknow was the president of Western Electric Company in New York City in the mid-1970s. This company, affiliated with "Ma Bell," was the equipment manufacturer for the AT&T telephone subsidiaries before they were broken up by the courts. Western Electric had a major plant in Oklahoma City.

I could have spent months trying to secure an appointment with Mr. Procknow by working through our local Western Electric management team. It's not that these executives held anything against me or the university—I'm sure they wanted to be supportive in every possible way—but the bureaucratic red tape and the constant "check-double-check" to see that all policies and chains-of-command were being adhered to would have driven a teetotaler like me to drink Jack Daniels. I had little patience for that kind of runaround.

Motivated by the old saw "nothing ventured, nothing gained," I called Mr. Procknow's New York office to secure an appointment. My favorite line (in this instance entirely true) was, "I'm going to be in New York City next week making some corporate calls and, if at all possible, would like to have just a few minutes with Mr. Procknow." My theory is that when setting up the appointment, the less said, the better. If they have questions, they can ask. On the other hand, if I offer too much information, I may give the gatekeeper just enough information to decline my request for a visit.

To make the point, I did receive the appointment with Mr. Procknow, who graciously accepted the invitation to speak at the university and at a luncheon hosted by the Oklahoma City Chamber of Commerce. He became a good corporate friend of the university, and the local AT&T management team was kindly disposed toward funding our programs for many years thereafter. Getting the appointment set everything else in motion. It was the most crucial part of my task.

Securing grants from foundations is half art form and half science. Careful research of the foundation's objectives, regulations, and restrictions can save us much time and money. On many occasions, our appeal simply won't fit within the guidelines of the foundation's funding objectives. Once we learn that, we may as well look elsewhere.

What's even more important, however, is to become acquainted with those individuals that serve as the foundation's trustees. Either knowing an individual on the board or having a common link to one of those trustees is the most important factor in determining whether you have much of a chance of getting a favorable response to your application for funding. With many foundations, the adage is true, "It is not what you know, but who you know."

Deryl L. Gotcher, the late Tulsa trial attorney and former president of the Oklahoma Bar Association, was chairman of the Oklahoma Christian Board of Trustees for almost twenty years. He performed well with the gavel, using his legal expertise to run an excellent board meeting. He and I had good chemistry and occasionally made funding calls together.

The J. E. and L. E. Mabee Foundation of Tulsa was one of the largest philanthropic institutions within our state. Their grants were usually restricted to brick-and-mortar projects within a six-state region, which included Oklahoma. Oklahoma Christian had received capital grants from the Mabee Foundation going back to 1963, eleven years before I became president. My job was merely to retain their goodwill and make periodic appeals for new capital grants.

Two of the Mabee Foundation's trustees in the Tulsa office were attorneys who held Deryl Gotcher in high esteem. What I found to be true over twenty years was that when I led with Mr. Gotcher in getting the appointment, we invariably received favorable consideration from the foundation. On those rare occasions when I tried to make the appeal on my own initiative, the answer was usually not what I wanted to hear.

People do indeed respond to people. Your cause must be worthy of the donor's attention, but, even with the best case, your chances of receiving a capital grant are enhanced considerably by having the right person help you get the appointment. If at all possible, they should also accompany you in making the presentation.

Making an approach to secure an appointment can be the most frightening task on our daily "to do" list. Fear of rejection haunts us as we rationalize why this may not be the right time to make this call. It's easy to move those difficult assignments to the bottom of the page where they are left unattended, waiting to be handled tomorrow. We may as well have a sign on our desk that reads, "Tomorrow is reserved for making appointments."

Time-management experts insist that we prioritize our daily tasks, being sure the most important matters are addressed before we zip through the items we enjoy doing the most. I have seen successful leaders set aside specific times in their weekly day timer exclusively for the purpose of making calls to secure appointments. Getting appointments is the lifeblood of any organization's future. As chief executive officers, we cannot allow ourselves to become soft in this crucial part of our development assignment.

Finally, when you are pursuing large donor prospects, place these high-level appointment calls yourself. There are times to use a secretary or executive assistant to set up less important meetings, but you will compliment your major prospects by being on the line the moment they pick up the telephone. Having them wait even a few seconds while your assistant gets you on the line is contemptible.

8

PAINTING THE PICTURE

A good case statement for raising capital funds, derived from a broad-based self-study, will put the president on the road to success; but that alone will not ensure that he arrives at the intended destination. It now becomes incumbent upon the president to communicate the message to those audiences that can do something about the opportunity at hand. The chief executive becomes the window through which the potential contributors view the institution, and the glass panes of that window must be perfectly clear.

Just because the president understands the urgency of the organization's request for capital funds does not guarantee the prospective donors will grasp the concept. The president must be an effective communicator, capable of painting the picture for all constituents. Moreover, the donors must be able to understand why these gifts are critical, and they must be motivated to respond favorably to the appeal. Without question, skill sets are involved in making a solicitation appeal, and some chief executives simply do not possess those particular talents. It may be at this point that they discover they have been promoted beyond their own competencies.

Perhaps Stephen R. Covey said it best when he wrote, "Begin with the end in mind." Potential donors need to see in their own minds the finished product and its value to the community. Sometimes that can be accomplished with well-chosen words. More often, it takes something more to convey the message.

One afternoon I made a solo call on Leonard K. Firestone at his office in Los Angeles. Mr. Firestone had spoken at a commencement program a few years earlier and had helped us with some small gifts toward an innovative educational technology system in our learning resources center. On this occasion, I was in his office to solicit a personal gift for the $15 million Enterprise Square, USA, project.

The conversation began with small talk: recalling his visit to campus, thanking him again for his previous gifts, and just getting caught up on recent events in our own lives. I liked him as a person, but I was slightly in awe of his celebrity status. Mr. Firestone, in addition to being a member of one of America's best-known industrial families, had served as the ambassador to Belgium under Presidents Nixon and Ford.

As I began to unfold the purpose of my call and the need for a capital gift, I began to sense that we were not tuned in to the same channel. At one point I caught him stifling a yawn, and I began to wonder if I was wasting his time and my own. Even among your friends, not every project will ring a victory bell. The thought passed through my mind to thank him for his time and not press the issue further.

To make matters worse, I had not insisted on having the meeting away from Mr. Firestone's office. It is virtually impossible to control the tempo of a presentation when you are a captive in the prospective donor's own workspace. The best I had been able to do was to get him away from his desk, but the deck was stacked against me.

Not one minute too soon, I asked Mr. Firestone if I could show him a designer's scale model of the proposed project. The best dollars I ever invested in a capital campaign were the ones spent to build a three-dimensional scale model of Enterprise Square,

USA, complete with detailed, artistic depiction of the various exhibits within the museum. The model was roughly twenty-four inches square and six inches tall, allowing it to slip into a protective traveling case that I transported all across the United States.

The moment I laid the feather board model of Enterprise Square, USA, on Mr. Firestone's coffee table, the meeting took a new turn. The captivating replica spoke to his heart in a way that I had been unable to accomplish with mere "sales talk." I have found that to be true with most people. Visualization is critical to potential donors responding favorably to any capital-funding appeal.

What I have also found, however, is that different projects, and even different donors, require different types of presentation aids. You, as the presenter, must be comfortable with what is being used. Just because some public relations specialist has seen a particular audio-visual aid work for another client does not necessarily mean that it will be right for you.

For example, I never was comfortable with table-top flipcharts. Some of my colleagues in higher education swore by them. I always felt that they made the presentation appear too contrived and made me feel as if I were just another insurance salesman.

On the other hand, I always insisted on the university's paying the cost for a colorful perspective rendering of any new building that was to be funded by a capital campaign. Elevation drawings have their place, but they are a poor substitute for perspective renderings when a president is trying to describe what a new facility will look like upon completion. If painted by an experienced artist or graphic designer, these drawings are well worth the front-end cost. They will save you at least "one thousand words."

At this juncture, you have to use your intuitive skills, deciding in advance of the campaign what audio or visual demonstration aids are required. "What exhibits do I need to help paint this picture?" Take the time to have these tools prepared before launching into a series of presentations.

I always liked to have my own quiver full of arrows and bring out just the right one for each presentation. If the call was being made on an individual donor in her home or office, I might choose to sit at her dining room table where we could spread out some drawings, models, or photographs. In some instances, a simple brochure or an oversized folio of pictures might help to tell the story.

A presentation before a foundation board or a corporate funding committee might require a totally different approach. In my day, it was a set of slides; today, it is the magic of PowerPoint or some other computer software that works best in these situations.

Of course, today there are so many spectacular vehicles to assist the president with his appeal. For example, the refinement of computer-aided design (CAD) programs now allows for a virtual tour of a new building before the first shovel of dirt has been turned. Coupled with a high-quality laptop computer, this medium can open eyes and pocketbooks of many prospective donors.

My only caution with "high tech" is that you not assume the audio-visual will do all of your work for you. You are still the master of the narrative and need to spend appropriate time in preparation of your comments. The PowerPoint cannot determine when an *ad lib* comment is required, but you can. Neither can the CAD program read the eyes of the donor. That requires the human element, and, upon that determination, the appeal may either succeed or fail.

When Dr. William S. Banowsky became president of the University of Oklahoma, I had the opportunity, on a few occasions, to watch him work his magic with potential donors. He had an uncommon gift with words and with his sense of timing. Few could resist his charismatic personality.

Dr. Banowsky's well-developed skill with people, as I observed it, was to make each person feel uniquely important while in his presence. "You are special to me," was the message that he communicated in a variety of ways. He also made each person feel as if there were a task that only he or she could perform, and that task needed to be accomplished immediately. Any visual aids merely helped to paint the picture. Dr. Banowsky, with his well-chosen words, was the one who created the all-important sense of urgency.

Not every chief executive officer will be endowed with the innate ability to read donors the way Dr. Banowsky was able to do. But it is important that you find your own way to paint the picture and create a sense of urgency with your prospects. They want to feel that their gift is needed and that it will make a difference in your efforts to succeed with your organization.

Sometimes the best way for a prospective donor to get the picture of what you need is to bring her face-to-face with your primary business product. A well-chosen student, for example, may be able to make the case for endowed scholarships better than the organization's president, regardless of how articulate he may be. A child from the Boy's Club or the children's home is likely the most effective ambassador that those types of organizations can find to carry their capital cases to their donors.

I rarely asked that students be fully scripted before making comments in a public setting. It always came across better if they spoke spontaneously, from their hearts. Some coaching with respect to general theme and amount of time allocated for their remarks may be helpful, but allow your "guest stars" to be as natural as possible.

On those occasions when you and your development officer are making a solicitation call together, be sure you have rehearsed the key elements of the meeting. Allow time at the outset for friendly conversation with the prospect. It is even advisable to spend ample time on the topics that are of interest to him or her as long as you do not lose control of the meeting. And be sure you know the answers to these two questions: 1) Who has the responsibility to move the discussion from friendly conversation to the fundraising issue? 2) Who will be making the actual solicitation request?

Finally, let me add a word about printed materials. Brochures, purpose cards, and leaflets all need to be printed with appropriate taste for the situation. Donors are turned off by shoddy workmanship in the design of these materials; and they are equally dismayed when they sense that their favorite charity has become extravagant in gilding the paper with too much gold leaf. Most campaigns require some type of printed materials. Your job is to see that they contribute to the job of communicating the message rather than becoming a distraction.

9

THE HIGH PRICE OF WORKING WITH LARGE DONORS

Securing a large gift for your organization can be the answer to prayer or the beginning of a nightmare. Occasionally, being the recipient of a sizeable gift may fall into that category of "be careful what you wish for." Don't misunderstand. We could all use more "angels" contributing sizeable gifts for our institutions. Before the celebration begins, however, there are some caveats to consider regarding large donors.

Personally, I enjoy the challenge of cultivating and soliciting those who can provide huge gifts for the charitable cause. Many of these donors are sophisticated in their approach to philanthropic support. They have been courted by talented leaders, representing all types of nonprofit organizations. Without doubt, we must have our "A-game" working in order to secure the million-dollar gift, whether it is from an individual, a corporation, or a trust.

Finding donors who are both capable of making large gifts and likely to do so can be a challenge in itself. Someone has said, "You will have to kiss a lot of frogs to find Prince Charming." They exist, for sure, because we hear of other institutions that are successful in receiving major grants. "Why didn't Mr. and Mrs. Jones make that gift to our organization?" we lament. There may be a host of reasons, including, "You didn't ask."

Large is a relative term. Michael and Susan Dell's $50 million endowment grant to the University of Texas was certainly a large gift. According to the press release, it was the second-largest grant ever received by the university. That tips the scale somewhere between large and *mammoth*.

At the same time, the $50,000 contribution a married couple tossed into the collection plate one Sunday morning at our local church was also a *large* gift. It was unsolicited, and there were no restrictions placed on the gift by the donors. That one check was four times the amount of the church's weekly budget.

Both the Dells and the anonymous couple from Horseshoe Bay meet the criteria for being considered large donors. And, as far as I am aware, neither of these generous families represents any kind of a problem for the university or the church. Believe me, it isn't always that way.

Tying Strings Onto the Gift

In the mid-1960s, while I was pursuing my law degree at Southern Methodist University, my predecessor at Oklahoma Christian, Dr. James O. Baird, was working on a capital-funding campaign to build a new auditorium for the college. The plans called for the new facility to seat slightly more than 1,200, allowing the entire student body to attend the mandatory daily chapel program. Most of the construction funds came from individual members of the college's church constituency and corporate donors in the Oklahoma City area.

The architect had designed the auditorium to have motorized, moveable walls, enabling the college to handle three large lecture classes simultaneously. Except for the hour reserved each day for chapel, the building was used heavily as a classroom facility. A number of the larger general education classes were taught in Hardeman Auditorium.

A popular federal assistance program known as a

Title III grant was created in that era to help "developing institutions" move into the mainstream of higher education. Since Oklahoma Christian graduated its first senior class in 1962, the college was an excellent candidate for this type of funding. The administration filed for a $50,000 grant (approximately 7 percent of the total cost of the building) to pay for the moveable walls that were necessary to make the auditorium function as a classroom facility. To everyone's delight, the college received the grant.

Two or three years later, the Title III auditor made a routine inspection of Hardeman Auditorium and saw the moveable walls that had been paid for by the grant. He noted a small plaque that credited the federal government with having participated in the auditorium's funding, and he also noticed the building being used each weekday for chapel. That's when the proverbial "fat hit the fire."

President Baird soon received a letter from Washington, DC, instructing the college to cease and desist from using the auditorium for any religious programs, especially chapel. Failure to comply would result in forfeiture of the $50,000 grant. Never mind that the federal money was less than 10 percent of the total cost of the building, or that its use was for moveable walls that made the building suitable for general education classes. Here was a donor that knew how to throw its weight around and was not afraid to do so.

It did not take President Baird and the college's Board of Trustees long to deal with the matter. They contacted their local banker, along with a few friends, and made arrangements to send the federal money back to Washington. This incident was a good lesson in dealing with a donor that chose to place strings on its gift.

Personal Favors and Undue Influence

Donors are like snowflakes; they are all different from one another. Some give from the purest of hearts; others cause you to wonder about their motives. If large donors begin to assert themselves as privileged patrons of the institution, life can become miserable for the president.

One such horror story was shared with me by a state university president who had secured a substantial grant from a widow who ran her late husband's private foundation. The gift was made to construct one large room within a huge, multi-storey academic building. Little did the president realize that his new donor—a sweet, mild-mannered widow—would become his new building's most outspoken critic. Nothing pleased her: the design was flawed, the materials were inferior, the workmanship was second-rate. Before that room was completed, the university had paid a high price for its big gift.

When a donor begins to make significant contributions to the organization, the question often arises, "Is this person someone who would be a good addition to our board?" Fair question. The donor obviously has interest in the mission of the organization or he wouldn't be making such large gifts.

But there is much more to be considered about nominations to the board than whether a person is capable of making big gifts to the operating budget and the capital campaign. Many of those who can give large sums are professionals or entrepreneurs who operate well on their own and are used to making things happen. The concept of "consensus decision making" is very foreign to them. They are accustomed to speaking and seeing others carry out their wishes. They are fish out of water in a board setting. If you allow them to do so, they will blur the line between the role of trustees and the role of management.

Besmirched By the Donor's Misdeeds

Occasionally, an institution can be injured by the bad conduct of one of its major donors. It's a simple case of "guilt by association." Colleges and other organizations have had the unhappy experience of taking the name off a building because the donor's behavior became a reproach upon the institution. Do you recall the name of the Houston Astros's baseball stadium before it became known as Minute Maid Park? Try Enron Field. Enough said.

Unhealthy Reliance Upon Major Gifts

Large gifts to the operating budget can make a president and his development staff appear to be doing their jobs in spades. After all, the budget is balanced and no one has had to break a sweat getting there. The team is congratulated for getting the job done.

What may be overlooked is how dependent the organization has become upon the large gifts of a few individuals or foundations. Take two or three of these gifts away in any given year, and there may not be a broad enough base of support to recover. All of a sudden, the budget is out of balance, and tough questions are being asked by the board.

If at all possible, direct all or part of large gifts to your operational reserve fund or to the unrestricted endowment. Let your operations be supported by the largest base of smaller donors you can rally for the cause. When smaller donors sense that their gifts don't really matter that much because Big Donor Jones is giving so much that the organization "really doesn't need my gift anymore," you are on a slippery slope.

Conversely, when small donors believe their gifts do matter, they have ownership and feel proud of their role in furthering the organization's purposes. This grassroots support is a valuable commodity for any institution. Solicit the large gifts, but do not let them be used in a way that lessens the interest others have in supporting your day-to-day program.

10

WHEN IT IS TIME TO PARTY

Nothing propels an organization forward more rapidly than those occasions when it celebrates its success. People like to be associated with winners, whether it's an athletic team, a political candidate, or a company whose stock is soaring. Celebratory events provide the opportunity for friends and donors to congratulate themselves for backing a winner.

Although there are many celebratory affairs that have little or nothing to do with fundraising, you would do well not to overlook the development angle of any public event. An employee's retirement party is a chance to invite his or her friends who will gain new appreciation for your institution or your ministry. Commencements bring wealthy parents and grandparents to your campus. Some will become your best prospects for an additional scholarship endowment.

Make sure there is plenty of sizzle in the event's program. For you, the homecoming or baccalaureate may have become routine; but for your guests, it's all brand new. You are sending a message about the institution and your own personal passion for its mission. Keep the energy level up and it will pay dividends when year-end gifts begin arriving in December's mail.

Some presidents have made the shortsighted mistake of downplaying their own inauguration. For a few, the decision was purely financial. They didn't want to put the institution to the unnecessary expense of throwing a big party. Others were embarrassed to host a ceremony that was focused so heavily upon the president himself. I understand that line of thinking and can remember toying with that decision.

Fortunately, an astute member of the faculty, hearing of my concerns, came to me and said, "This is not about you! This is about the institution. Every organization needs to find those occasions when it can celebrate its past and project a vision for its future. You must not take this opportunity away from the campus community." Looking back, that inaugural event was loaded with development potential. The money we spent to host the convocation, along with the dinners and receptions, paled in comparison to the financial gain we realized over the ensuing years. Decades later, generous donors reminded me that they were present on inauguration day. They caught the vision of the college and measured the cloth of its new chief executive.

When a funding campaign comes to a close, some type of concluding event is required. Volunteers need to be thanked for their efforts. Leaders need to receive tangible gifts that generously express the institution's appreciation for their service.

This is the time to be creative. Find a gift that is well suited for the donor or reminiscent of the campaign. The best example I can recall occurred at the dedication of a new fine arts building. When construction began, Oklahoma red clay was dug from the site in order to prepare for the building's foundation. That very same clay was sculpted into lovely pots and vases by one of the art professors. These pieces of original art were glazed, fired in a kiln, and presented to the donors at the dedicatory event. They expressed gratitude better than any words etched onto a brass plate and attached to a wooden plaque could possibly have conveyed.

Celebratory events can eat up enormous amounts of staff time in the planning and execution stages.

This is a good time to draft some volunteers that can become an extension of your development team. People love to plan a party, and some of them are better suited to that task than they are for anything else you may ask them to do. Two cautionary suggestions: 1) Maintain control of the event; you will be the one judged by its outcome; and 2) keep the "development card" foremost in your mind so that you have no regrets about having let a cultivation opportunity pass you by.

On a picture-perfect Oklahoma morning in March 1992, Oklahoma Christian University hosted President George H. W. Bush in the outdoor bowl known as the Thelma Gaylord Forum. Fifty or more Bradford Pear trees were in full bloom, welcoming the president and almost a hundred members of the National Press Corps. There was not a cloud in the sky, and the Oklahoma wind, as if on cue, was remarkably calm.

Our advance notice of the president's decision to come to Oklahoma City was one week. Immediately upon hearing the news, committee sessions were called and assignments made. A wooden stage structure had to be built for the speakers' rostrum and a substantial staging area for the press gallery. Secret Service agents came days in advance to survey the grounds and determine if sight lines could be adequately protected. Screening stations were put in place so that every one of the seven to eight thousand attendees could pass through metal-detection devices. Nothing was left unscripted.

Going through my mind was the thought, *What a coup for the university.* For the first time in our brief history as an institution of higher learning, a sitting president was going to be on our campus. Key donors were asked to join us in the VIP seating section near the front of the forum. Mr. and Mrs. Edward L. Gaylord, by far the most influential family in Oklahoma and good friends of the university, were asked to join Marty and me, along with our student body president, Jeanetta Davis, to welcome the president when he first arrived on campus. This was a "pull out all the stops" kind of occasion.

The university band played, the chorale sang, and representatives of the athletic teams lined the stairway where the president and other stage dignitaries entered the forum. The president gave a rousing speech, and even the press appeared to like it. A spectacular Associated Press photograph covered the front page of *The New York Times* the next morning. The entire event was a president's development dream come true.

Reflecting upon this event, I am overwhelmed by the man-hours consumed by staff and volunteers to make this day the memorable occasion it turned out to be. And even though some costs were reimbursed, the day was expensive! But rarely does anything this good come without cost. If you are going to throw a party, make it a good one. The little extra it takes to go first class is usually a good investment.

———

When I interviewed for my first job at Oklahoma Christian, having completed my law school degree, I told President Baird that I would be willing to assist in administration but wanted to have nothing to do with fundraising. He smiled, redirected the conversation, and offered me the position of staff counsel. Little did I realize how much I would enjoy the onerous task of asking people to help support a worthy cause.

A president who cultivates a taste for fundraising is light years ahead of his colleagues who struggle with the assignment every day of their tenures. I share these thoughts and experiences with you, hoping that you will find your calling more enjoyable with each passing day.

I quote my friend and mentor, Dr. William S. Banowsky, who has often said: "If you can bring together someone who has financial resources with a charitable organization that is honorable and worthy of their support, you have done a good day's work." I like that thought. It has inspired me during those times when funding was slow or when I have overheard someone say under his breath, "I'm glad I don't have to beg for money to make a living."

Hold up your chin. Stick out your chest. Someone is about to say yes to your next request for a gift to fund your institution.